PRECIOUS
MOMENTS
TO
TREASURE

I0203242

By

Precious Arnold

PRECIOUS
MOMENTS
TO
TREASURE

Milino Publishing
Detroit, Michigan

PDA Management
Redford, Michigan

June 19, 2010.0013
Milino Publishing is a division of thee Faith In GOD Ministries
ICOA

MILINO PUBLISHING-PDA MANAGEMENT
ISBN 978-0-578-05587-9
Precious Moments To Treasure
COPYRIGHT© 2010 / 0013 AD / AO BY PRECIOUS ARNOLD
Printed in the United States of America
ALL RIGHTS RESERVERED

PRECIOUS
MOMENTS
TO
TREASURE

PRECIOUS
MOMENTS
TO
TREASURE

Thank you

First and foremost I would like to thank GOD, knowing the journey to success is a challenge given to us as a test. Thankful for all that has overcome me, bad has improved me.

There's so much in so little time to put into words. This book is not only my thoughts but feelings that are straight from the heart. God is the one who would never let me down. As a young child I was taken through a lot, but being shown a way to open doors for myself and others, I'm standing strong. My family and friends has given a lot of support. I'm thankful knowing God begins your day and ends your night.

Loving free, living life as it's given to me, my mother Angela and Grandmother Juanita which are my biggest backbones, helping me through it all. There are so many people that have helped me, I say thank you to all of you.

To my Dad Clarence, Granddad RV, uncle Chris friends D'eandre, Ravinne, support from the fans at PDA and also importantly Tommy Bray of Milino Publishing, who helped make all of this a reality.

Counting my blessing daily Gods my witness.

Precious Arnold

PRECIOUS
MOMENTS
TO
TREASURE

PRECIOUS
MOMENTS
TO
TREASURE

Contents

Dedication

Chapters

Moms feelings gone wrong
My Angels from above
Beautiful death
Moms understanding
Little things
Wondering why
Outlook
Hoping
True wishes
Destination
Life's Handful
If only
Missing fear
Stephon
Game change
Change
Past view
2 Young

PRECIOUS
MOMENTS
TO
TREASURE

Chapters

PRECIOUS
MOMENTS
TO
TREASURE

Moms feelings gone wrong

I hate to see you cry,

I hate to see you ask god why.

I just hate to see your pains which really aren't remained.

You forgive and forget but over and over again I see you in pain,
Which I hate so much and he loves so deeply

I see your pain; I feel your love,

I think so hard on how much I hate your thug, he does you wrong,

Treats you bad

You know what that man has nothing on my dad.

<u>My Angels from above</u>

God sent me two angels from the heavens above,

I can't think of life without my two loves.

Every step and move they make I'm sure to be there.

The angels are more than life but a beautiful blessing
from the joy of having kids.

I have wished for angels for so long and now that
they're in my life I never want them gone.

<u>Beautiful death</u>

Everyday someone dies, every moment someone
arrives.

That one day I'm going to die and never come back,

Death is a strong word of no life or joy.

Some people say death is freedom,
But just that one day I guess I will find out if death is
joy or just a word that mean's I'm gone.

When I think about death I think of taking my last
breath.

I think about not being in this world but just going with
the wind, free of all sins, pressure and all hard times.

Death is freedom, love is pain, pain and love is what I
got for my family.
Love of freedom, is a strong word.

Pain is tears, tears may fly, tears may dry, but my
feelings and my words will never die.

<u>Moms understanding</u>

Mom you are a sweetheart from heaven.
I love you so much that I don't know where life would
go without your flow.

You have been there from the day I was born
I'm sure you will be there when I die.

You stay by my side even if I do wrong.
I don't understand why you hold on so strong.

I love you more than life itself.
Wondering how a beautiful lie can seem to be forever
Lasting

Never seeing God step to give me more
Knowing there will never be a replacement.

<u>Little things</u>

It's the little things you do that make me happy.

It's the things you have been through that makes me wonder why.

You make me think what a good life is and what a bad dream is.

I say, If only the little things you do could return a perfect nightmare.

I searched for so long and found the key to the little things, are the success to great things.

<u>Wondering why</u>

My life is ruff, like really bad.

I mean what can I say when I really don't have my dad.

I think on how much I love somebody I don't really know.

If just that one day he would come in and I'll just let all this stuff go.

I really don't understand what's really going on or
What really happened, but
now I can't wait for that one day I meet my dad.

<u>Out look</u>

I love me for me and hate me for the things I do.

I see how people think on my life as if I got it all.

A beautiful cover up

I try to do right but I always end up doing wrong!

Life seems to be a dark spot, that terms has no
definition other than the wrong.

Letting others believe in outside appearance, but a torn
apart inside thrown out they don't see.

Knowing life is spare change of differences and no true
definition.

Hoping

I'm always thinking about you even though I tell myself
not to, I still do.

Night to day you're still in my thoughts, I try to think of
something else but I think of you instead.

Just too many memories I could never forget I try to tell
myself this is it.

All these thoughts have got to end.

I try but still I have feelings for you I can't pretend.

This is something that I need to face, because I know
these aren't feelings I can just erase.

I need to tell you how I feel and everything I tell you
are for real.

True wishes

Life is ruff, times are bad.

I think on how much I know I need my dad.

I never know, I never will

The thought hangs on my mind,

How much I love my dad that I never had.

Love is in my mind when I see this invisible man

When I hope and with one wish,

Before the end I can meet my dad.

<u>Destination</u>

When I think to myself I don't want to be here.
I think of the freedom that may appear.

I hope to help when needed while I'm here but still have
that thought of not wanting to be here.

When I think of taking my last breath I think of the fear
of making my last destination of the free press.

I know that's wrong to have the hope of not waking up
when I know that would mess up a lot of lives.
Specially my freedom of joy my baby boy!

<u>Life is a handful</u>

Life is what hurts

Pain is a part

Feelings are what we get

Trouble is a second half

The joy is just a fear

The seconds on the earth are treasures

Moments in which time can't destroy

In pulling all of this together makes me.

<u>If only</u>

If I can see my father just once

A change of fear
Not too long

Just a moment to spare

Noticing how a beautiful dream

Quickly turns into a nightmare

Wondering how one doesn't feel to share

Knowing there's more to a story than a person's wild
fear

Hurting to just see a normal dream clear

If only I could meet my father just once in life if only

<u>Missing fear</u>

I was missing what I once had
But I still have to think twice
On what I got now.

Love me now
Hate me later
Please don't take any more heart breakers away from
me.

I never really thought I would be here
Put in this place of guilt and fear .

But know that I'm blessed
To even have to be loved to the fullest

You were what I thought I had,
But now you're in my past,
I am put in the future, love n missing fear of regrets.

Stephon

A person in the mist of the lost,
His life mistaken from the start,
change for a child Estranged.

Gifted to a healthy family
Mother missing the best understanding.

Hope for the lost to-be found,
He's not just a boy; he's my brother, a great
Part of my heart, from the same mother yet
Separated from the start.

Worth waiting to meet my Angel,
Saving a few years to get a great understanding

Forgiving a mistake, but never forgetting he's an
important part to my family.

A little man with a confusing past.
Identifying pieces that seem to-be torn apart.
Never giving up, my love is forever lasting.

A sister blessed to know there's always
Someone to look forward to meeting.
Angels aren't always handed over, you have
To put them in as God has them cross
Your path in life
Guilt that there's nothing in my past,
Could change my present.

A one-way street down to my blessing.

<u>Game change</u>

Just when life gets a lot better the hope in the game
change

When I thought I was taking my last breath, something
hit with a final answer of what I wanted out the free
press.

The joy jumping high and the play stand low.

For all the fought and heart breaks came and may come
I lay hopeless in pray.

I found out it's called the hope in the game that may
remain.

<u>Change</u>

Hoping one day comes to good endless moments.
Wishing or praying is all I have a choice of doing.
Maybe one day I can change or reward my past in a
outstanding way.

Hoping to open a door to a brand new life but no one
knows what that would ever turn out to be or time as
being if there's a chance to relief.
When I pray it is forever not for the devil.

The angels that showed me to love is a beautiful effect.
God took me to the red carpet, held my heart and told
me use it wisely of precious moments.

I could never get enough love to take my breath, just
enough to see a different life just a beautiful day.

Everything happens from left to right what's wrong with
just being between.
It hurts to know what's done in the dark always comes
to light.

How will I ever forgive?

Will we ever be right?

Who said I believe who said,

Who thought life was right.

God gives you another chance now it's your turn be a different man.

You said you love me with open hands.

I took to you with a broken heart.

You had me thinking you were something I wanted

Something very different inside and out!

<u>Past view</u>

How can I change your past will you ever be the same.

When things go bad how do I know the real name.

Now she's in your past let's not forget my name,

A beautiful thing of a moment to remain

The one who love you and wishes to be true

Do you lose a good thing and be so stupid you put me in pain.

Just never put your heart where your mind is,

You may fail a beautiful dream.

Always remember my name a valuable gift to hold on to in your heart

<u>2 young</u>

My life is turned around when wrong,

I'm happy you gone,

I'm ALONE again, I thought you were perfect

Everything was really so wrong.

When my mind goes to a state that has nothing to do
with you,

Some reason you call out why.

I thought life was perfect, but can't find out how.

Love is what I thought you had,

But I guess I'm to young 2 understand.

But I'm sorry for being the dumb one to trust in you.

You're now in my past and that's where you belong, all
alone.

Love is a beautiful dream,

A women's wild thing,

A man's harmful way of pain,

A dark side of a human being,

Out look outside a fearful wing,

A stream of a health vain,

Pain healing steam,

A wonderful thing,

Nightmares wildest light,

Stride for a bright sight,

My behavior in a different life!

<u>A big difference</u>

My thankfulness I'm still here.

I see you in my dreams there's no fear,

The sunlight is bright and my nights are dark,

My days and seconds are slowly coming apart.

I wish to see another day in hope to pray for the great
love ship passing over.

I give it some years in we will have our family, I just
can't wait to overcome our fears.

A daddy I never had is there for mines as a father not a
sperm donor.

<u>Missing feelings</u>

I miss your face.

I miss your hugs.

Now you're gone, I still have your love.

Days go by, clouds high and strong.

My boo is now gone

I have seen your face bright and light up with things
very wrong.

Now I see nothing but the words he's gone.

The time is here when you're at home, with god above,
on

Cloud 9!!! 15 years old and strong

<u>Right and wrong</u>

Just when you were right I went wrong,

Just when I got strong you were gone,

Can we ever take a step forward?

How will we ever move on?

The day I thought I was grown,

You were there when hell hit strong.

The angel I seen wasn't there, she was with you when the day I

Seen wasn't able to be shown.

I'm looking ahead but I see no one above my love.

A dark dream

A beautiful nightmare,

A dream with a deal of no fear,

Loving ones successful dare.

Heartless to the worthless thing called pain

Thankful for the moment of the vain

Wondering the worth of feelings,

Hearing the hope of willing,

Time isn't spared or giving

Seconds in life's minutes.

Terms of hours that's forgiving

May never be promised the breath at the ending

Thanking God

A child with a second chance at life,

Who's fear maybe at sight?

Mother may never seem to care,

My dad is a dark nightmare

Wisdom to be successful,

A beautiful little girl to the world

Open door to the floor, a start at hand

A beginning with gods ending

Daring to be different, loving the chance to be who I
am.

God's child is a blessing to those lives with a passion.

A chance to be me

Believing in a fear a beautiful nightmare,

A dream with no ending, wishing to see something
different Hoping to be successful,

Being the person I am inside and out.

A heart full of joy endless happiness, loving and
treasuring Moments of destiny

A gift of the brightness, precious answering to the
wrong and right

Value the true sign of spite, seeing nothing new but
very clear and blue.

Opening the door to the light, letting one shine in my
life without the right

Loving the true gift of just being me, blessed because its
life I live happily.

<u>Loving all the wrong</u>

Those who are wrong will always,
Seem to be strong

There's a way to be placed on a throne,
When time seems to move on,

Loving the wrong,
Leaning to hold on

Preparing for the worse,
Knowing time is a lot to embrace

Crying because you're feelings hurt,
Willing to stay because this is where your heart lay.

Believing you deserve better,
Chance to change your life forever

Life's gift

A present of life itself,
Thankful for life's time

Sorry for the time it hit,
Knowing it's a gift that can't be for rent.

Wanting to give one your all,
Believing there's a reason for wisdom.

Hurting because love is strong,
Knowing there's no turning back I may never be wrong.

Feeling there's a reason for everything,
Seeing how God presents things.

Trusting nothing but above,
Reliving the faith of love

<u>Worth while</u>

Finding out the truth
Loving your past
ahead to the future to fast

Trying to be the best while time is given,
Being a person who's well willing
Daring to make the biggest difference
Seeing the true feelings aren't expected,
Points to the worse,
That the truth hurts.

Hearing one's lies and knowing the feeling,
Life's what you make it,
It's your chance to deal with it or better yourself without
it.

There's a proven statement a beautiful liar,
A person with wisdom to make a difference,
A chance at hand

A proven fact isn't just the one's you love,
But the one's you can't seem to live without,
Proven fact love is a dream welcome to reality.

<u>Faith</u>

Hearing the truth,
Knowing the facts,
Life's a hardship to pass.

Not sure which direction to turn,
All the time seem to overcome,
Seeing your life at night's dark.

Days seem to fall apart,
Moment's worth to spare,
Now there to fear

Reality is wisdom,
One's true feelings,
Known to make a change

Wanting to see things more clear,
If there's a way around the hurt,
Always told what don't kill you can only make you
stronger
,
One's word to life in a try to god is to make life a place
to treasure, always and forever

My blessing

A baby girl to the world,
A promise to heart,
A future star,
A making to a break,
Love of my life,
A little human being,
A angel God's gift,
A fear to protect,
A dare of difference,
A little girl to history,
A beautiful act,
A attitude to guard,
A chance to have meaning,
A wonderful little sister with God's blessing a faithful
reason!

<u>A missing feeling</u>

Giving one a chance,
Not willing to feel daring,
Loving them but having mixed feelings.

Changing in a way of not caring,
Believing its life,
When it's a bad call god lets it be known whether
you're happy or gone.

A father to a child I may never really know,
A chance to be something I never had,
Now he's here you let me go.

I'm not just watching your actions but the things that's
being done, Hurting no longer,
Learning in life people come in and leave a tear.

Can't hold on to something that was never yours,
I put it in God's hands and just let go.

A father's, role something I seem to have never had,
But glad a little boy got to get in a place where I
thought I belong so now I'm strong.

Mistakes that could never change

A heart full of loving someone you let go,
A chance to become someone you always dreamed,
A fear that may never change you let go,
A past that could never be the same,
I let love slip away.
A beautiful thing something not everyone can maintain.
A angel to the world,
A star to history,
A mistake that will always stick with me,
A thing that life has given me,
I didn't take it properly,
Instead I live now with guilt,
Now the one that could've changed my life forever,
Has now been seen in my past with a future never
Pain is a strong thing,
Overcoming seem to never change,
October 10 will always be the same,
The love of my life a beautiful dream

Careless

Becoming who I am,
A person who's bare,
Attitude from hell,
Worse feelings of fear,
Sharing nothing but tears,
Knowing I'm alone while I'm here,
Wanting to move on,
Seeming to be so strong,
A background of a book on my own,
All of a true story,
Christian faith in soul,
Has a lot to carry,
Changing only in spite,
Heart is cold,
Hearing words that never means nothing,
Caring for myself and scared,
Thinking maybe it's only god calling from the start,
Dreaming that I'm home,
Awaking to a careless life that seems to depart

Difference at life

Spare change of wisdom,
Fair difference,
Waiting for a change to explain my department,
Seeing all that is asked is patients,
Willing to give my all in a second,
Wishing things could be different,
Life's times spared but mostly given,
A mind of a man,
A hand to hold,
A heart to warm,
Fear the end will be the dare of not willing,
Knowing a person's kind at soul,
Spirit that will always seem gold,
Ones true feelings on hold,
Killing a dream, Daring a future,
Loving one that seem to always spare the difference,
Faith at ones strength,
Mind that one's breathe could easily be taken away,
My good luck charm could never really see his
meaning,
Me wanting that much more for life a huge difference,
Soul that may never come to be him again,
Hurting knowing life's what you make it, what's his
difference.

<u>Open chance</u>

A man with a great hand,
A loving heart,
has the right to give you a brand new start,
Making your past history,
Letting your future be a key to things,
Successfully meeting the means of dreams,
Hurting that the one I love is a person on hold,
Things that have happened to me don't stop me,
That's a way to inspire me,
A day to myself of thinking brightly,
A moment to give thanks to ones that always had
something against me,
A heart to lock a key,
A.J means a lot to me,
Changing only if it means living freely,
Tired of crying for a father that is a far distance of me,
Needing no one but god above,
Hearing him when it's my time to go,
Looking to make a move,
Far from stress,
Depressed never less,
See life's change in front of me.

My love

I love my mother,
A Beautiful human,
Technology of a woman,
Give a chance at life,
Seeing a angel,
Separating good,
Departing bad,
Never wants to know her child's at harm,
Staying next to me at my worse,
Yelling because she cares,
Me knowing I'm always first,
Wanting to hand me life,
Giving me options to be a child while I can,
Maybe a little too hard,
Despite the fear of love,
Holding on to me at a close heart to soul,
Seeing her child make a difference,
For feeling dreams,
Acting of not caring,
Wanting to know her child's every move,
Thinking the worse of the silent voice,
your child knows at the end of life given time itself I
always see you first .

Is love to much to ask for

I sit back in look at my past refilling the future.
Wanting so much more,
I try hoping for the best to many coming between the
progresses.
Wishing to have just one more breath or a movement
with a share of heart,
Thoughts go through the air but will never blow
through.
Wondering how many life's will be changed if together
we could be .
Place together away keepers,
Reality between love and hate,
Caring less of what people really think.
The best that could ever happen came so quickly,
By time going on it drifts away slowly,
My love,
My heart,
Beats because your swag so cold
Believing it's me and you against the world.

I love my mother

Your life is in God's hands and mines in hell.
Am not saying I'm not happy just not where God place
me from the beginning.
I really hope you live to see what you want me to come
out to be.
I want to walk across the stage and see you with a smile
of just being proud of your child.
I really hope I make it where I need to be before the
sunset end and am not going to be happy.
Memories aren't for me I just want to be gone before
you make your decision.
Having to be so unhappy wouldn't be good for me.
I mean really you're all that means the world to me.
Speaking of a gift to me
A mother who's really a shift of pride
Brightness of a night to clear the fright
Your Kisses as fresh as the sea,
Your hugs as tight as can be.
I always want you to be happy.

<u>Feelings about daily life</u>

I see how much time I take to tell you how I feel are
you really worth all the time I give,
Wanting more than just that show of a role you play,
Deny nothing I'm truly loved,
Sure the colors I wear don't describe my outlook.
Family and friends are all of my makeup .
Morning and night thinking of survive,
If life was without you,
Working on a shift that seem to never end,
Growth of a child
Blossoming of my minds brightness,
Taking life this far to never look back,
Forward is ahead of my time,
Past is never to repeat.
Wrong couldn't be changed,
But easily forgiven
Without so many and the support,
Couldn't stand this high,
Strong and gifted
Seen and been given a change of life background,
Chapter after chapter here,
Of an unforgivable feeling

Love

Love is a beautiful dream,
A woman's interior strength.

Terms of nine months that applies
To make a difference,
A stream of healthy little veins.

Love is a beautiful thing,
Some men ways of harmful pain,
A dark side of a human being.
Feelings that are easily exchanged,
Between happy and pain,
Smiles between tears.

Love is a beautiful thing
Nightmares wildest light
While striding for a brilliant sight,
On behalf of a good life!

Is love to much to ask for?

A place within happiness,
A reality between love and hate.

www.ingramcontent.com/pod-product-compliance
Lightning Source LLC
Chambersburg PA
CBHW032036090426
42741CB00006B/835

* 9 7 8 0 5 7 8 0 5 5 8 7 9 *